Games like Skylanders: Trap Team *can hold kids' attention for hours.*

What Is Online *Gaming?*

1

A boy's character enters Containment Corner. He's playing in chapter 13 of the online game *Skylanders: Trap Team*. Skylands' most-wanted villains have escaped from Cloudcracker Prison. The boy's character is a Tech Trap Master. He must work with other Skylanders to trap the villains. The Mabu has given him a "villain quest" for Wolfgang. He easily captures Wolfgang and continues the quest.

Some online games are played on computers. Others are played on **game consoles**. They are even played on **mobile** devices, such as smartphones and tablets. Some are single player games. Others are multiplayer. These can be played with friends.

Many gamers enjoy playing offline video games. Online gaming, however, is much more popular.

Gaming online lets people far away play together. Millions of players can join in a single game at the same time. This makes online games appealing to many players. Computers and consoles are often used for online gaming. But mobile gaming is the most popular.

60 Percent of online gamers who play mobile games.

PUBG Mobile is a popular online mobile game. It has more than 1 billion downloads. • Gaming on computers is more popular than console gaming. • One of the first mobile games was called Snake. It was available on phones in 1997.

Fortnite can be played on a mobile phone.

Esports are just like a real sports match, but people play video games instead.

2 What Is Console *Gaming?*

A video game console connects to a TV. The players use game controllers to interact with the game. Gamers also can use other accessories, such as joysticks and steering wheels. These make gameplay easier.

Video games can be played offline and online. Not all consoles need to be connected to the internet. But most features, such as downloading new characters, require an internet connection. Players might choose to play offline if they do not have an internet connection.

Others may enjoy playing alone instead of with other players. However, many console games are designed to play online. Consoles connect to the internet just like a computer. They use the same network. Gamers can play with people around the world.

Some controllers can be attached to steering wheels or joysticks for a more real-life experience.

Console games require you to buy each individual game you play. You can buy a physical copy of the game. It looks like a DVD. Or you can buy a digital copy through online stores. However, it is possible that digital copies will not transfer to future consoles.

ARCADE GAMES In the United States, few arcades still exist. Arcades are places where people go to play video games. Each game is played on its own large machine. Today, arcades let people experience games the same way their parents did. They played games such as *Street Fighter II* on a big machine. Today, people play similar games on small smartphones.

What Is PC *Gaming?*

3

PC stands for "personal computer." Players use a computer to play online PC games. Most online players prefer PC gaming to console gaming. Computers have more power. Games tend to run more smoothly. Computers have better **graphics**. These make games seem **realistic**. Game creators often want games to look as real as possible.

Some PC games are more difficult to play than others. Real-time strategy (RTS) games are played live with other players. All players move at the same time in an RTS game. This makes the game more complicated to play. The action moves quickly. Gamers need to work together and make quick decisions.

PC gamers can buy a month-to-month subscription for some games. A subscription gives players access to all of the game's content. Free-to-play games let players try a game for free. But often, players must buy upgrades to use better features. They might see more ads too.

14,535 Number of new games released in 2023 on Steam, a digital game store.

There are about 3 billion gamers worldwide. • About 1.86 billion gamers play on a PC. • Around two to three game developers work on a PC game.

Almost all esport competitions are played on PCs.

THINK ABOUT IT

Would you enjoy playing online games on a console or a computer? How would interacting with other players change your gaming experience?

PlayStation 5

What Are the Different Types of *Online Games?*

4

Gamers can play video games designed for either single players or multiple players. A single-player video game allows people to play alone. Online games are usually multiplayer. They let gamers play with others over the internet. Millions of people play **simultaneously** in a massively multiplayer online game (MMO). Some MMOs include voice chat. That way, players can talk to each other while playing.

One type of MMO is a role-playing game (MMORPG). In them, millions of people play together in a single game. They create their own characters. Characters start with few skills. The goal of an MMORPG is to grow your character. Players build their skills. This is called leveling up. Many MMORPGs, such as *Wizard101*, take place in a fantasy world. Others, such as *Overwatch*, are set in the future or even space.

Link is the main character in The Legend of Zelda.

1986 Year the first *The Legend of Zelda* adventure game launched.

The world's best-selling video game is *Tetris*. • In 2024, one of the most popular types of gaming was shooter games. • Simulation games let players do things such as dance or play sports.

Another type is adventure games. These let players discover their own **virtual** world. Players solve puzzles and collect valuable items as they game. In a shooter game, the goal is to shoot objects. Players face enemies or obstacles. Simulation games allow players to have real-world experiences. Players perform a physical task on screen but not in real life. Some games allow players to build cities or entire civilizations. There's a game for everyone.

FIRST OF ITS KIND

In 1984, Nintendo released a game called *Duck Hunt*. It was the first of its kind. To win, players used an accessory called a Zapper. It was connected to the console by a cord. The player aimed the gun at a TV. They shot at the ducks on the screen. Inside the gun was a sensor. It detected light patterns on the TV. It could sense if the player shot at a target.

Old Nintendo console with a Duck Hunt *cartidge*

TECH SMARTS

12 QUESTIONS ABOUT ONLINE GAMING

BLACK RABBIT BOOKS

MARYSA STORM

Table of Contents